THE LIFE AND ADVENTURES OF WILLIAM REID

SECOND EDITION

WILLIAM D. REID

WORKBOOK PRESS LLC
187 E Warm Springs Rd
Suite B285 Las Vegas NV 89119 USA

Website: https://workbookpress.com/
Hotline: 1-888-818-4856
Email: admin@workbookpress.com

Ordering Information:
Quantity sales. Special discounts are available on quantity purchases by corporations, associations, and others. For details, contact the publisher at the address above.

Library of Congress Control Number:
ISBN-13:   978-1-963718-29-4   Paperback Version
              978-1-963718-30-0   Digital Version

REV. DATE: 03/12/2025

THE LIFE
AND
ADVENTURES
OF WILLIAM REID

WILLIAM D. REID

WorkBook
PRESS

INTRODUCTION TO MY BOOK

As far back as I can remember I always wanted to
Be a writer like my grandmother, because of the happiness
I saw that it brought her. So through my growing up years whenever
I watched my Grandmother sign books for people who'd come visit
her, it hit me one day! How would it be to do the same thing in my own
life. Meet people, autograph books, and be in the
spotlight. Here's a quote I'd like my customers to think about:
"I love what I do,
And I do what I love"

CONTENTS

A DANCE WITH DEBBIE

December 12, 1981

I went to a dance one night
And danced with lots of girls,
But there weren't very many that
Really did much for me.

But one in particular person
Which I was afraid to ask of her,
Just take time to dance with me.

And while we were dancing
To the slow music that was playing,
It was like being in love again
With Debbie in my arms.

Revised October 30, 2013

A DAY IN MAY

May 29, 1979

A day in May as there are
So many days in May,
But this was a particular one.

It's supposed to be warm
And sun shiny bright.
We should have had this weather
In March not the end of May.

We had been moving pipe
On this morning my uncle and I,
So when I got through with my line,
I noticed how cold the weather was.

And the wind was blowing so hard
That by the time I got half way
Down the second line of pipe
It had begun to snow.

I couldn't believe the kind
Of weather we were having
For that time of the year

A DEATH IN THE FAMILY
December 20, 2013

It seems as if all my old friends
Are now pert'n near all gone,
Who were friends of my mom and dad,
And in the association they belonged.

There were several different families
Over the years I'd gotten to know.
One of these was the Butler Family
And these were Bertha and Woodrow.

Well, as the years go by like they do
Their kids and I became friends,
We would see each other on the range
And then go home at the day's end.

Always when we would be going
On our way to the hills or back home,
Dad would pull over and talk to someone
Because in those days there were no phones.

As we were all getting older now
And Casey took the Butler girl for a wife,
I'd known her brothers for some time
But was very glad they came into our life.

Whenever there was something going on
That all of the families would go to,
Including Weddings and Anniversaries
I would go talk to the people I knew.

We were always going to other funerals
Of People we'd known who had passed on,
But I was very surprised when I'd heard
That my friend, Woody Butler was gone.

A FEW GOOD TIMES WITH MY FRIEND MIKE

May 8, 2015

I've been lucky to have had a few friends throughout my school life, and most of my adult life as well. The one here in particular is my friend Mike. We go back a long ways. So now we had been out of school for some, time. He had a job in Idaho Falls at one of the restaurants where the people he worked with knew both of us. After having worked there for a while, along with his dad, I would ask Mike's dad if we could go do something. Which, of course he didn't have a problem with.

We often went to the movies where there was an outdoor theater in Idaho Falls. Other times we would go to the Virginia Theater in the town of Shelley where my friend Mike grew up. But when we weren't, you could find us at his work, or just hanging out. After a while of getting to know Mike's dad, and to the point where I wasn't afraid of him anymore; we would go other places. One of these was Yellowstone Park. So I called Mike's dad, and asked his permission to see if it would be alright if I took Mike to the park for one weekend. He finally granted my wish after I sat down with him to discuss a plan for being back home. This done, before we left I had given Mike's dad Gerald a time frame that we would try to be back by.

Now Mike and I could get started and were on our way. Saturday night we pulled into a place called Island Park, and got us a room for the night. This was back when I still had my little yellow truck, and my dog Brownie that went with us. I always paid for everything including, meals, the room, and even the entry fee to get into the National Park. Come Sunday morning and a good night's sleep later, we finally made our way in the park. As soon as we could we drove a short distance, just to let Brownie dog out to walk around for a few minutes; so he wasn't confined to only the pickup bed. From here we would go enjoy ourselves, and see as much wildlife as possible before heading back home.

After having been in the Park for a while, I decided it was time we get out of there and start heading towards home. And now that we were on our way home, we would eventually pull over to get something to eat, then hit the road again, and get Mike home as quick as possible. If I remember right we did get home at a pretty reasonable hour. It was a long time after that before I dared ask to take Mike anywhere again. But on one of these occasions, I did just that! In the first place I didn't see any harm in taking Mike to Pocatello zoo, and Old Fort Hall, upon the hill above the zoo, its self.

The one thing I didn't know that was going on in the town of Pocatello was a 100 year celebration. All in all, it was just another day to us, until we were walking back down the hill, and watched the steam engine train pull, into Ross Park where it dropped off our Governor at that time. This was Governor John Evens. My friend and I did not have the opportunity to actually meet him, but we saw him from a distance. To my knowledge this was the summer of 1982. I know Mike enjoyed himself even if he didn't talk much, that day. And once again we would take him home.

A FISHING STORY
Originally Written in 1975

My brother Paul and his wife
Went fishing one day
And took their dogs along.

The dogs left for a while
Then pretty soon came back
And knew something was wrong.

When up on the bluff above them
Was a cat that was big and furry
After they had spotted her
Away they did hurry.

So down the river they went
And never did go back
Because the winter before when
My brothers went snowmobiling,
They thought they'd seen some tracks.

Paul's wife Billie thought it was
A bobcat of some kind or another
But she doesn't know animals very well
Near like Ted and Paul, my brothers.

It was a Mountain Lion that they found
And she probably let out a loud scream,
Since this was just a warning for
Paul and Billie to go back down stream.

They thought she might have babies
By the way she acted that day
But they weren't about to stick around
And find out anyway.

So home they came and told us this;
I have a wonderful story to tell you
But we didn't catch any fish.

Revised April 4, 2005

A STRANGE COINCIDENCE

July 10, 2008

I remember when my brother was dying
From a second stroke he'd had
That put him in the Hospital awhile
And that's when things went really bad.

Well, a couple of times I went up there
And ran into someone I knew
And said, what's going on Old Friend?
That is when he gave me the bad news.

He said, Bill "I lost my brother from a
Heart attack he had the other day"
As I was listening to my friend Rolland,
I told him, I'd lost a brother too,
The very same way.

In all the times I went to the hospital
To meet my family and to see Ted,
I just had a certain feeling about;
My brother wasn't coming back to life
Because he really was dead.

I would see Rolland in the waiting room
And talk about our brothers like we did
It was hard enough just losing them
But we both know we will see them very soon.

Revised Jan 11, 2015

A STRANGE THING

March 12, 1979

A strange thing happened
To me one time
When I went for a job interview.
We had been in the office and had
All the paper work done.

Then the secretary was asked
To show me around the place
So I gladly went with her,
To the area where I'd be working.

Here she'd explained to me
The kind of work I'd be doing.

So after we made the rounds and
We stopped outside the office,
She hadn't yet told me her name
But was getting ready to.

When somewhere out of the blue
I had this funny feeling I couldn't explain
That had a message in it for me
And it told me what her name was.

Right at the time she was
Going to tell me,
I had already read her mind.

It was something from
Outside our five senses we have
And far beyond our reach.
I'd never experienced such a
Powerful and unusual strange thing
In all my life.

Revised October 30, 2014

AMERICA'S BICENTENNIAL WAGON TRAIN: 1776 – 1976

September 22, 2013

A lot of different things were going on back in the 1970's. For one Expo 1974 would happen, and eventually my younger sister get married; but this would be in another story. The biggest thing that would happen was America's Bicentennial. While there were many celebrations going on all over the United States, the one that I would remember for the rest of my life was right here in Idaho.

Well, as of the dawning of the 1970's I would meet different friends that my dad had throughout his life. I was lucky enough to have the privilege to work for this old timer, who'd been a long, time friend of my families. I was very grateful that this old pioneer gentleman had asked me to work for him. This was the winter of 1973 and the beginning of 1974.

While I was staying with Frank I felt like I learned a lot from him. Two things I would remember for the rest of my life happened while I worked for Frank. One of these things was the loss of two former Presidents which I remembered one of them very well. The other would be a story that happened during the late 1890's that Frank liked to talk about. It's just kind of odd how certain people make a lifetime of memories in one's life.

Another friend that my dad had was a very interesting kind of fellow in a different kind of way. I'd always envied people like him all my life. One reason for this was, it seemed as if he had everything going for him. Mr. Green had some of the most beautiful horses a person could own. After all, he had a wagon to go with them, and was always doing parades, or showing his fine horses off somewhere.

Sometime back I remember I had seen something in our news paper, about a modern day wagon train, that was going to start at Swan Valley; and would take about three days to get in to Idaho Falls, just like the good ole' days. So I talked to my parents about going up there and check it out anyway. And we did, but it seemed as if we no more got there and the wagon train had started on its way. This was probably the first time I remember of hearing about a wagon train in my life time.

A few years would go by now, and we would be in the biggest celebration of my life. America's Bicentennial. I'd been going to 4th of July parades and Labor Day parades, as far back as I can remember; but this was different. Our Country was turning 200 years old, and to celebrate that many years of Freedom is a big thing. For one thing our regular circulating money would change for one year at the U.S. mints in honor of our country's birthday. And the U.S. Treasury printed 2.00 dollar bills with the Revolutionary War Founding fathers getting ready to sign the Declaration of Independence on the reverse side of the 2.00 dollar bill.

Also the Winchester Firearms Company had their own way of celebrating the Bicentennial year, with limited editions available for the general public to buy. I don't know when or how dad's friend, Zaven Green, got contacted in order to be the person to represent Idaho for the trek across the United States. I was so glad when I'd heard about this, because now mom, dad, and I could make plans to go see the wagon train at its beginning point up at Ross Fork.

For one thing this was right on the old Oregon Trail. We finally got up there, and the first thing I noticed was how nice of a day it turned out to be. While Dad and I were getting acquainted with the Oregon and Washington wagon masters, Mom brought her camera so she could take a few pictures of this once in a lifetime event. So before we broke camp we got everybody together by Mr. Green's wagon. From here the folks and I would come home, and the wagon train on its way to Washington D.C

.

Rewritten April 30, 2014

AN OLD COW
August 17, 2011

For many years I remember
An old cow my Uncle Fred had,
And every year at branding time
You didn't dare make this cow mad.

So after rounding up the cows
The way us kids always did,
Then help trail them to their destination;
And corral em' where they
Would be fenced in.

Now that the cows were in the pen
The easy part of the job was done,
We still had to separate the cows
And watch out for the mean one.

Because when we would separate
The cows and calves in the pens,
You really had to be on the lookout;
Or this old cow would chase you until
All of us were upon the fence.

A few years later I had learned
That Uncle Fred had sold this cow,
That caused us kids such a problem
I was really relieved somehow.

BRANDING TIME HELPING UNCLE FRED
August 13, 2012

Back when I was a very young lad
A certain story comes to mind,
When we were rounding up my uncle's cows
And it was right around branding time

Well, we got them rounded up alright
Down in what we called the lower field
Then headed them towards Uncle Fred's place
But I was getting the short end of the deal.

Everybody had a horse of their own
While I got stuck with a useless old nag,
And in the meantime we were moving the cows
The horse I was using became more of a drag.

The other cowboys were helping trail the cows
While the horse I had dumped me off on my head,
They were getting in on all of the fun
While I might as well have been left for dead.

As I was laying on the ground in unconsciousness
A whole different world appeared to me,
The brightest light I'd ever seen in my life
And a strange figure of a man stood before me.

So as I was coming out of the state of
Unconsciousness and seeing stars,
The first thing that I noticed was
The herd of cows wasn't that far.

After I'd rounded up the old nag
That I'd been riding for the day,

Then help Uncle Fred corral his cows
Like we always did in a neighborly way.

Eventually we'd have something to eat
Since this was the reward for us kids,
Then go back to work dragging the calves;
To the fire, the way all of us kids did.

This is what we usually did before
We would head the herd up the big trail,
After combining all of our cows together;
Which we did many a times
Regardless of what kind of weather.

BURIED TREASURE STORIES

March 29, 2015

All my life I've heard stories about buried gold caches from various people I knew, including distant relatives of mine who live in La Grande Oregon. We were always going to go back up on the hill above their place, and try to locate that treasure, but never got around to doing so. I'd done a lot of research and acquired all kinds of books on the subject, for many years. I even talked to other people to see what they might know that I didn't.

Even though I had all this reading material available to me, it would take some time to make sense of it all. The most important thing here was, I would be looking for buried treasure stories that dealt with Idaho. In the first place, that's where we lived, and the proximity of where one could look. In all the books I bought I finally found a few local stories that started to make sense to me.

A book called Robbers Roost seemed to be the most accurate of what I was looking for. It even included a small portion of Idaho, and mentioned an 1896 bank robbery in the town of Montpelier, that was close to not only the Wyoming state line, but Utah as well. Throughout the years, and over time, many things would change. One of my cousins would get married, and live in that neck of the woods for a short time.

However, a couple of years would go by before we wound up down there for a deer hunt. This is when my cousin Rich asked me if I wanted to go. So I said," yeah sure, why not." At least it gave me a break from the farm. As soon as I could get ready we would head through the Mountains and be on our way to stay with Tom and Wendy for a couple of days. The next day we got up and ate some breakfast before going out on our hunt. We drove for a while until Rich, and Tom, decided it was safe for us to start hunting.

While we were out here in the wilderness we did get our game we went out for. As for me, when we finally decided to come home, I'd have a different memory for the rest of my life. There was this huge incline if I remember right and only if you were a goat, or a horse, you could probably make it to the top of this hill. Well, in later years after I'd worked potato plants for a spell I got to know a few people who'd grown up in the area, where I'd been sometime back.

Now I could start my investigation. In later years after working for J.R Simplot a while there was only one person I knew who was from Montpelier. This would be Dianne. So when we would work together throughout the day, or week, I'd ask her about any buried treasure stories she might have heard around her family circle when she was growing up. And much to my surprise she had. For one thing, she got to hear these first hand experiences from her Grandfather.

The next question I needed to ask Dianne was did her Grandfather know of any buried treasures in the area? And she said yes he did." As I'm listening to my friend here relaying these old stories of long ago, I'm quite intrigued with them. First of all I learned a lot from all of this. The Grandfather had actually found a gold treasure back in the day. And to me, it sounded like it was up that big hill where we had hunted, or nearby. But to my knowledge, even though the old man knew where the treasure was he never made an effort to bring it out. And the granddaughter, my friend Dianne, told me the same thing.

DONETTA AND MARY CAN'T

January 30, 1985

All this time I have loved you
I've only asked a few things,
To be a responsible person
And to keep the house clean.

But no matter what I've asked of you
Either you can't or don't want to,
Which I don't know but if things don't change
I'm going to have to let you go.

You could do it if you want to I'm sure
It just seems to me that you can't
And would rather walk out the door.

It seems as if neither of these
Partners of mine wanted to be a wife,
So all they ever thought about
Was going and messing up our life.

Either you can't or don't want to
Which I don't know, but if things don't
Change I'm going to have to let you go.

You could do it if you want to I'm sure
It just seems to me that you can't
And would rather walk out the door.

FAIR TIME

September 1978

A time to remember is
When two friends part,
After having good times together
It seems like we just got started.

There will be other times I'm sure
When we will be together again,
On holidays or weekends would be
The only time we could spend.

I loved every minute of it
While we were at the fair,
I went on a few rides with them;
And I'd never felt any better
Than to be with good friends
Like Teresa and Diane.

The night before they left
To go back to school,
Teresa gave me a big kiss
That I'll always remember.

One that said good bye
But I will be back soon,
It may not be right away
And it kept me from being blue

I walked with them as far as the gate
Along with another friend,

Since that is where we parted
And went our separate ways.

Diane was already out the gate
Before I could give her a kiss,
Teresa is the first girl that I'd held;
In my arms in a long time
But Diane will never know what she missed

Yes, a time to remember is
When two friends part,
After having good times together
It seems like we just got started

Revised February 15, 2005

FEELING UNWANTED

May 24, 1984

It looks like it's over
Between us I guess
Mary and Donetta know how
To say no but not the word yes.

All I've ever asked of you
Was to just be a wife,
And not go and mess up
Our whole life.

I need you more and more each day
I ask you please let's not drift away.
I ask you with a pleading heart
I loved you from the very start.

The things I did, I did for you
Because no one else for me will do.
Come back baby let's try it again
I know in my heart,
It will be right in the end.

Rewritten Feb 4, 2014

FRIENDS

September 29, 1978

All my friends are special
To me in one way or another,
Depending on the person of course.

Because there aren't two people
Alike with the same personality,
I ought to know that much or more.

For I have friends all over the country
From California to Northern Idaho,
And from Home to Alaska.

Yes no matter where I go
I'll always make friends with someone.
I don't know what it is about me
That the people like so well,
Probably the same as what I like them for.

I'm a friendly type of person
Anyone would tell you that much, and
I get along well with other people;
And the same goes for them.
But not always!

GENTLEMEN

Circa 1974

What we need in this world
Are more romantic men
The Romeos the Casanovas
And even the Virginian.

They all knew how to treat
The ladies and greet them with a smile,
And when they had to leave again
The girls knew that it would be a while.

But the day would come when they
Would be back again,
They didn't know what day
Or month or just when.

But they would greet them
In the same old way,
Like it was on that very special day.

Revised May 20, 2014

GIRLS

August 15, 1978

The feelings that girls have
Are so very tender,
But so are some men's.

You have to be careful
And watch what you say,
Or we might take it wrong;
And won't know what you mean
Until you explain to us.

We are very sensitive people
And it doesn't take much to hurt us.

Revised November 2, 2013

GOD

Circa 1978

We think of him in spring time
With flowers everywhere
We think of him at Christmas time
When joy fills the air.

We thank Him for each season He brings
That we might have life through the Holy King.
We should thank Him for each day and night
And be glad that He gives us light.

Jesus tells us He is coming again
But so many people don't know when.
Maybe it's because they don't understand
That Jesus is trying to lend a helping hand.

In Rev. 3 verse 20 Jesus is saying
Behold, I stand at the door and knock,
If any man hears my voice and opens the door;
I will come in to him.

Well, the door is man's heart and by confessing
All of our sins is just a start.

We think of him at Easter time
When Christ arose from the dead,
We give thanks to God at the Thanksgiving time
For the crops and everything we did or said.

Revised August 11, 2014

HALLOWEEN NIGHT
Fall 1980

I'm only Wild Bill once a year
So the rest of the time,
Have no fear.

I'm not really wild like I say I am
I could be George or I could be Sam.
Who found their Gold
Up in Alaska where it gets very cold.

I'm not really wild like I say I am
I'm really quite mild,
And most people don't
Know me any other way.

I may not be Wild Bill
As you have seen,
It only comes once a year
And that is Halloween

Revised May 10, 2014

HAPPY 15TH BIRTHDAY BRITTANY

August 18, 2011

Happy Birthday to my youngest girl
Who is going to turn fifteen,
I don't expect much from you now
After all, you are still a teen.

As your Father, I do care
What happens to you, you know,
I know you don't see things this way
But you will the older you grow.

You can't say I haven't been there
For you with all the games I've been to,
And they weren't just for our school,
They were also for you.

I know you don't see me as a Father
And for both of us that's sad,
Now you know what I went through
All my life with my Dad.

So, Happy Birthday to my Little Britt
And from my heart this I mean,
I know you don't think much of me,
But maybe later in your life,
This will remain to be seen.

JACK AND ED

September 21, 2008

Sometimes I see a couple of
My friends in town that I know,
So I'd sit and have breakfast with them
Instead of just saying Hello!

It's hard to say how far back
In time our friendship goes,
Especially with these two friends
Ed William's and Jack Mitchell.

Both of these names were well known
Around our local community,
And every time there was a school function;
My family made sure I got to go.

I knew the William's Family very well
From going to school with them,
Linda was in my class at school
And I'd known her brothers Ray and Edwin.

Jack's family has always been
Real good friends with The Reid's,
And if you ever needed a favor done
They were the ones to call on indeed.

This was very true later in my life
Because Jack's brother had a body shop,

And two accidents later my wife had, had;
So one day when we were out doing nothing
By Derryle's place we decided to stop.

While we were over here chatting
About the situation we had at hand,
And my family was very familiar with
Derryle's work as a body and fender man.

I don't remember how long
I've been going to breakfast with Jack,
So we just made it a tradition
That's why I keep going back.

JOHN AND THE BAND

January 2011

There is so much in life that describes all the people I'm going to talk about in this story. Right after I moved back to this area, and that would be May of 1979. And I had nothing better to do except hang out with John and his Band on weekends. Once again I had a guaranteed job working for my dad and brothers, but I would only go out on Fridays and Saturday nights. Well, one of the places I'd hang out was where John and his Band played music on the weekends, at a place called Stan's Bar and Grill, in Blackfoot Idaho.

It's kind of hard not to remember everyone in the Band, and they were always glad to see me. Sometimes when they would be in the middle of a song the drummer, Nate, during the song El Vira, would go El Vera. So whenever the Band sang this particular Oak Ridge Boys song, this is what I remember most about Nate. Besides playing in the Band, these people had regular jobs during the week. Heavy Duty (Wayne Hale) worked for the City of Blackfoot. As for John, Nate, and Arkansas Eddy, I never knew what line of work they were in.

John and I probably became the closest of all of the band members. I would go support them on weekends, and in return they gave me something my own family didn't. This is called encouragement. But the thing I remember John the most for is a little jingle that he and the band used to play called "Working for the Yankee Dollar". Where the song came from I don't know: Maybe Arkansas Eddy, or John wrote it, but I'd never heard it until I started to hang around John and the Band.

How Arkansas Eddy wound up clear out here, in Idaho, I didn't have a clue. But one thing is for certain here about everybody in this story. They just

43

fit together like a puzzle, so I believe that without Arkansas Eddy, the band wouldn't have been what they were; but the same could be said of any of the band members. Sometimes when the band weren't playing their music John would come over where I was playing pool and shoot a few games with me while they were on break. This way I got to feel like I was part of them.

John's wife Sandy, worked at the Bar where her husband's band played music on the weekends. However, she was a full time bartender all week long. Many times I remember when there was a full house, and if the girls who worked for Sandy serving drinks got a little bit behind, Sandy was right there to help out. In all the time I've known Sandy, this is the kind of person I saw her as right from the beginning, a real sweetheart of a gal. Mrs. Hale, on the other hand could be found hanging around on the weekends, as well. After all, she was married to Heavy Duty. During the work week Mrs. Hale worked at a local bank in the town of Blackfoot Idaho.

Most of the time when the band was playing, they all had their favorite place where they liked to stand on the stage. So when a person came in from the back door of the bar John was the first person one would notice. Then Heavy Duty in the middle, and Arkansas Eddy on the end, and of course Nate; the drummer was always ready to pound out whatever song the band decided to play. Sometimes Heavy Duty would play the banjo, other times the mandolin, but most of the time he played the guitar. I always liked it when he did play the mandolin because of the sound of it I guess.

LOOKING BACK

Circa 1974

Over the years as they
Seemed to have gone so fast
I'm one who's often looked
Back into the past.

The days of the Stage coaches
And the Pony Express
Even a Saloon girl
Wearing a pretty dress.

Rewritten January 14, 2015

LOVE

August 10, 1979

What is real love?
We all ask ourselves
From time to time.

We all have a general idea
Of what love is,
But does anyone know
Until they have been shown.

Love is caring for one another
And understanding one another.

Love is what brings people together
As friends, or partners, or otherwise;
And love is when someone cares enough
To say are you alright!

After getting up from a chair
And nearly falling down
Because one leg was asleep
So you could hardly walk.

Then you brace yourself on
The nearest thing in front of you,
Until you are able to walk again.

Real love is what more woman
Show me than any guy can.

God has shown me what love is
By associating with women,
Whether married or unmarried;
Because I love them just the same
For being what they are. Women.

Revised August 12, 2014

LUCKY THINGS NO. 9

November 4, 1975

They say a horseshoe is
A very lucky thing,
Like the girl who
Wears a diamond ring.

Marriage is only the beginning
And death is the end,
Because diamonds are
A girl's best friend.

Diamonds are forever you know
For every year you live together,
Another diamond glows.

Revised June 11, 2014

MARRIED WOMEN

October 7, 1978

I seem to always get along
With married women more,
Than I do the single ones.

Maybe it's because they
Understand me better and,
Know what I'm looking for.
Sure I'm attracted to them,
But only as a friend.

Yet there are a lot
I would consider marrying,
If they weren't already.

A married woman is probably
The best friend I have,
So whenever I have a problem;
I usually talk it over with a married woman.

Rather than talk to a guy,
Or a single girl since they don't understand me.

Revised March 12, 2014

MOM'S 97TH BIRTHDAY

December 11, 2012

I can't believe we are about to have
The biggest birthday of our life,
That will bring the families together
And to make Mom feel good as Dad's wife.

It seems as if only yesterday
That they celebrated seventy two years,
I can't believe where the time has gone
With most of us siblings still here.

But the birthday we're about to celebrate
Not too many people get to make,
And say they lived a good long life
Or get to light 97 candles on their cake.

Mom has been one amazing person
That no other person can compare,
Especially when it comes to playing cards
And what she needed, happened to be there.

Yes, even at our mother's age
She still finds things she can do,
Making her candy or baking bread
She seems to always come through.

MRS. TAYLOR

May 27, 1979

Through the years I have known
Mrs. Taylor to be the best teacher,
A student could ask for
Since she was good to me.

She was so good to us kids
All the years we had her,
Which was quite a few;
But I was glad we had her
Before she said adieu.

She was the main foundation of
Our life and taught us kids to read and write,
So we could go on without her
But she was never out of our sight.

If it hadn't been for her
I wouldn't be where I am today,
And I'd like to believe that she is;
The reason and would give me her ok.

I had a lot of teachers after her
But none that I could compare,
With the one I remember the most
The one with the pretty red hair.

If a student can't respect a good teacher
From the time they got one,

Then it's not what is the matter with
The teacher, as it is with the student.

Now I've been out of school
For nine years, thank God for that!
Because I hated our last teacher
Who has nothing but a dingbat.

Rewritten September 26, 2014

MY FIRST GIRLFRIEND

May – December 1976

I had a girl friend at one time that I liked and truly loved. The first girl I'd met since I had been out of high school. My cousin and I went bowling one day when she just happened to be there. So I asked her if she and her brother would bowl a few games with us. Which,of course, they did.

I liked her more than anyone I'd ever been around. I'm still good friends with her and I see her every time I'm home. It was love at first sight for me, but I can't say for sure from her point of view. It probably wasn't the same until she got to know me a little better. We would do fun things together regardless of what the weather was doing. There is no way you can split us up since the feeling is still mutual between us, but only as close friends now.

The first time I saw her was in the spring time. I was working for my uncle at the time helping him cut potatoes for the farmers. We were way behind on our jobs we'd been doing, but had caught up some; so we could go home early one night. So while Wallace and I were on our way home we liked to have a cup of Russian tea. Whatever was left over from lunch time, sometimes it would be a little bit, other times a lot. After we got home I cleaned up and went out on the town so I could see this girl; until I decided it was time to go home. I would take her home and talk 'til midnight sometimes, even later than that; before going home myself so I could be ready to meet the day.

I'd taken her out a few times now, and while I was working I would get this funny feeling in my stomach during the day. It's plain to see that I was having butterflies, and this had never happened to me before; but I knew what was going on. I'd never felt that way about anyone, just this specific girl. That is when I knew I was in love with her but I don't think she ever had the same feelings for me. If she did, she never expressed them.

Here I was a twenty five year old man who had been hunting for a woman at least two years. And when I thought I'd finally found one, the only one who has understood me; better than close friends I had and more so than my own family.

We got to know each other's families very well. One time when I was going to town, I got pulled over for speeding. I wasn't really in a hurry, even though it may have seemed like it. This was the first time I'd gotten a traffic ticket since I started driving a car. I was going in to pick up my girlfriend since it happened to be my folks 40th Anniversary at the time. A special occasion once a year that my family was good at celebrating, whether it was one of Dad's brother's birthdays or whatever the case may be.

We had gone dancing the night before and had everything planned for the next day. My folks Anniversary is on a bad day anyway: It's the same day as the President of The Southern States Birthday during the Civil War, Jeff Davis. So I was bound to have bad luck that day. After getting a ticket I'd never had in my life I started slowing down more than I ever had before. I remember one time in the park we went way around to the other side so we could be alone, and talk for a while. We weren't really doing anything wrong, but guess who decided to show up anyway! Around where we were parked.

A city patrol and it took him a while to figure out that we weren't doing anything. Anyway he took his own sweet time about it, and I bet he was there at least five minutes. As for me I didn't dare move other than to look behind me in the mirror. Whenever I had something to say I'd tell Donetta not to talk to my folks, but to talk to my sister in laws; if she ever had something to talk about. I had my reasons for not wanting my girlfriend talking to my parents. One was because they didn't understand me. The other was I couldn't tell them anything.

Donetta and I went bowling one time and she could tell that I was a little slow. This was before she ever knew anything about my medical condition that I was born with. The funny part about all this was it made no difference to her. And it was something that we could both over look, since it wasn't that big of a deal. She'd been in basically the same situation I had been in, back in my younger days. There were times when I thought I was bad off because I didn't have a car. Later I found out from her while we were going together that she was a very shy person and never went out when she went to school. I guess she had her share of problems too, at least from what she has told me. I can't explain how I felt about her the first time I saw her, but I knew I wanted to be with 'er somehow. And being shy as I was at the time I sent my cousin to ask her and her brother to come down where we were bowling.

That way I could get acquainted with her then decide whether I wanted to see her again. As it was when we got through bowling I wasn't sure anyway. This was because of my cousin Cliff, better known as the little Indian; nearly scared Donetta and her brother away. I don't exactly remember how he got the nick name but I do know my family was famous at that. It didn't matter who you were in the family, my Uncle Fred or someone else would find another name for you.

About a week or so later, after we were there the first time she and her brother Dana came back to the bowling alley, which was a big surprise to me; since I didn't expect to see her right away. Here I was across the room from her and thinking to myself; things aren't supposed to work that way. But one time they did. Now I knew I wanted the chance to be alone so we could get to know one another, rather than having other company along.

We compromised all the time. First we would spend some time with her family and next time we got together we'd spend with mine. Her folks are very nice people and some of the best I've ever met. My girlfriend's mom worked in a restaurant for a while and learned to do almost everything there was associated with the business from cooking to waitressing. I don't remember how long her mother worked for the restaurant but she has been taking it easy for some time now. Donetta's dad was a spray pilot all his life working for the big shot farmers in Winnemucca, Nevada. He even had his own plane and kept it at his place of business where he would stay all summer. I guess he made pretty good money but I don't know for sure.

I was invited out to dinner one time down at my girlfriend's house where she grew up in town. We had a really good time and I got to meet her younger sister, and her husband. I didn't even know Donetta had a younger sister until that day when we sat down to have dinner. I remember one time we went to visit her Grandparents that lived on the outskirts of a town called Blackfoot. I think we were there for a dinner sometime during summer of 1976 just to get acquainted with her family.

There was another time also that same year where I met her mother's side of the family and other relatives. While we were there throughout the course of the day between eating, socializing and what not, it seemed as if everyone enjoyed themselves. After a big meal which we just got done eating everybody was sitting around the dining room. Her Grandmother's place was so crowded that there were not enough chairs to go around, so I had Donetta sit on my lap.

It was alright for a while until one leg went to sleep then I'd have her switch sides so I could stretch out the one she'd been sitting on. Throughout the course of the day I remember a comment her dad had said, that had something to do with me. Right off hand I don't remember what it was but I didn't like it. Somewhere in the midst of all the commotion her dad Joe had mentioned something about if she wanted to go home with them or not.

I have to say it sounded like a good idea at the time but I decided it wasn't such a good idea after all. I think she knew I didn't want her to go home with her folks, this way I could have the pleasure of taking her home once again. That's what I liked best of all so we could be alone, and talk things over. It was like we belonged together somehow and something I hadn't ever experienced in my life time.

I am one person who will listen to other people whenever they have a problem that they need to talk about and get off their minds. So if either of us had anything to say the other of us was always willing to listen. I asked Donetta once if she would like to go up in the Mountains for a picnic. So she packed us a lunch and we went for one weekend, up where my Grandmother's cabin was.

Well, in the beginning the old cabin had remained on the homestead from when it was built in the early days. And over time, different forms of irrigation changed throughout the course of people's lives to water the land. Nobody knows more about this than my family. Starting with my Grandfather, and then my dad all his life chasing streams of water all day long.

After the first pioneers had settled here in the South Eastern part of Idaho, my family would be one of those who decided to make the Blackfoot River Valley their home. And in doing so, my Great Grandfather Nels was always looking for something to do. During the time that Nels and Emma lived on the land they homesteaded he noticed they needed a way to get water to the land in order for plants to grow. From what I understand Nels was a great promoter and anything he set out to accomplish he did just that! Including the building of two ditches to carry water down, stream. One of these canals was on the outskirts of a town named Eagle Rock, but later would be renamed Idaho Falls. The canal once it was completed became the Idaho Canal. So now the Upper Snake River Valley had water and could irrigate the land with a shovel for the time being.

On the other hand we still didn't have water but eventually we would, because of a project Nels Just was working on a few miles from home. One thing is for sure in this situation. My Great Grandfather needed men to work for him. And my Grandfather was just lucky enough to help build the ditch that would carry water to the valley for irrigating the land.

By the time my generation came along, the way we watered the land had changed dramatically the last fifty years. Even though my dad for many years I remember would get up early go chase water and set canvas dams on the lower part of the land. My three older brothers were learning to move pipe. This would be the farm land up on the hill. How this operation worked was you had a pump in one part of a ditch in order to send the water through a pipe line and then you turned it on at the top of the main line.

In order for this to work it had to go through a process, and a lot of hard labor. My younger sisters and I usually got stuck with the job! Our dad would tell us to go find one of the tractors that wasn't being used, then hook up the pipe cart to it; and haul these sections of pipe back across the 40 acres of land and start over. At this point one of us would have to drive the tractor while the other two of us unloaded the trailer, the pipe were on.

Each individual section had its own sprinkler on it, as well as a hook and latch system to connect them together. By the time we got to the bottom of the hill where one of dad's fence lines ran, we had probably covered a quarter of a mile from top to bottom. At least we had a job all summer long that kept us busy, and when it was over we would go back to school. Yes, us younger siblings had to learn to move pipe too. Over the course of time that the old cabin sat on my Uncle Wallace's land, it was just rotting away. One reason for this was, it sat right in the way of the sprinklers, in the middle of my uncle's pasture. From here my family would move it to the Mountains and rebuild it. So one summer that is just what we did for all the family to enjoy. Here is a poem that my grandmother wrote about farmers and irrigation:

"The Man In rubber Boots"
By Agnes Just Reid

In the land of irrigation
Where the desert blooms as a rose,
There dwells a knight in armor
Whom everyone loves and knows.

He guides the little streamlets
To the famishing stems and roots,
He carries life in his shovel-
The man in rubber boots.
He doesn't write great sermons,
Nor argue points in court,
He doesn't rush to battle
And he has no time for sport;
But just to be near to Nature

He leaves all other pursuits
And spends his life in the open,
Deep in his rubber boots.

The river out in the valley
Where man has scarcely trod,
Keeps calling, calling to him
To till her virgin sod;
And the song of the river is music
To him as she cries for recruits,
So he hurries away to her service,
Shod in his rubber boots.

Sometimes when we quit shouting
Of braves in battle slain,
Of Lusitania victims
And those lost on the Maine;
Perhaps we'll sing some praises
To him who reaped no fruits,
But made the waste an Eden
By toiling in rubber boots.

Besides using the water for irrigation, we used it to play in also. One of these things was swimming. The other was for floating down the river because, that is what we did in our spare time. So during the summer while I was trying to get to know Donetta, I also tried to interest her in what we did for activities around the farm. I would even invite her to go swimming with us every time the family went. I don't think she had any idea of how much it upset me and especially when I was hoping to see her in a two piece swim suit a few times, but I never did. I'd talked to her about it before and asked her what color swim suit she had, which of course she replied blue. This really took me by surprise since most girls choose, red or yellow, or some other color than blue.

In August when my Grandmother had died I was down at my girlfriend's house where we had been talking for a while. Then I decided I would see what was in the News Paper. So I thumbed through it and found this write up about my Grandmother. I was very surprised even though I shouldn't be; where my Grandmother had been fighting cancer for a long time. I don't think Donetta or her mom had a clue that we were even related until I told them. Also Donetta's mother mentioned something about my Grandmother that made me wonder how she even knew. So I asked her mom but I don't remember exactly what she told me.

Most of the time when I would go visit at my girlfriend's house I'd spend a good share of that looking at the fashion catalogues on the table. What I would look for was a gift to give her at Christmas time. She would look at them with me which is what I wanted her to do. This way we could scan the pages together and pick out something, we both liked. It was late summer going on early fall and my cousin Rick was going to get married for the second time. In doing so my family would be invited to the wedding. So when I knew this was going to happen, I asked Donetta if she would mind being my date.

I didn't know for sure if she would or not, but anyway she gladly went with me. I will never forget the night of the wedding, when she wore her pretty blue dress. Before the wedding ever came about I asked her what color dresses she had. Then she mentioned a few that were hanging in her closet, that hadn't been worn since she was in High School. I just said wear the blue one and that's what she did!

Rick had been married once before to a girl everyone knew in our local community. So my cousin was getting married for the second time in his life. The girl he was marrying, I really didn't know anything about; but it seemed as if all the family approved of her. During the summer my dad's youngest brother Wallace and his wife Marlene would celebrate their 25th Anniversary. After all, they were the ones I wanted her to meet, most of all. We'd already celebrated my parents 40th, and through a big shindig for them. This was back in June when Donetta got acquainted with all my Aunts, and Uncles, on my dad's side of the family, plus all my cousins.

It would be September before we were able to celebrate the big event. By the time the actual Anniversary happened My Girlfriend I had would meet a broader spectrum of people, I'd known all my life. A lot of these were in the Cattleman's Association that my dad, and uncles, belonged to. So we rented the High School Auditorium on the Saturday that was their Anniversary, which was fine; because the people of the district knew we always cleaned up after having a party. This is the way the Reid Family has always done.

There were so many people at the party that I don't remember all of them. But the ones I do recall were the older generation. The room was plenty big for all the family, and friends who showed up at the rendezvous. Even though I had a girlfriend with me I tried to make sure my elderly friends were taken care of. The people who wanted to dance, could dance, and the people who wanted to eat; could do so. Eventually the party would come to an end and everybody would go home. The one thing I'm sure of is, we all had a wonderful time for Wallace and Marlene's 25th Anniversary.

My girlfriend and I liked a lot of the same things. I liked to go bowling she did too. I also played pool and tried to teach her. So when I'd take her out to my folks place we would go down stairs to play pool in the basement of the house I grew up in. But we usually didn't since we were a card playing family. I tried to get Donetta interested but she hadn't played anything except rummy. And the game we liked to play all winter was pinochle. This is what we did for entertainment.

When summer came around and we had spare time my family would play baseball. So one time when I brought my girlfriend out home I got her to join in our softball game, even though she was a bit hesitant at first. We got along and everything but we didn't always agree on certain situations, then of course no body does. We went to a movie during the summer at an outdoor theater because of something that was of interest to me. The title of the movie was called, Buffalo Bill and the Indians. Paul Newman played the main character in the movie. I'd seen him in several films, but I wasn't sure about this one; portraying Buffalo Bill. He did better than I thought he would.

My girlfriend and her mom got along quite well, and sometimes it pays to have a good mother, daughter relationship. However, when she had a problem that she needed to talk about; since I couldn't always be around she usually went to her mother. I couldn't talk to my parents in the same way my girlfriend was able to with her mom; because no matter what I did I could not please them. There were a few things that I could talk to the family about, but mostly not. So I would go to one of my sister in laws since I knew they would understand. It's all really very simple because, I wanted to talk about sex, which I would never bring up around family. They wouldn't tell me anything, anyway when I was growing up.

Thanksgiving was coming up soon so I decided to call my girlfriend a few days before to ask her if she would like to come out for dinner. So whilst we were on the phone she did agree to spend part of the day with my family. After dinner we went out to her Grandmothers place and spent the rest of the day out there. It was a month from Christmas and I was still wondering what to get her. Looking through the fashion books every time I went to see 'er, I would ask all along what she wanted. By the second week of December I'd made up my mind what to get her. In the meantime, I told my girlfriend she could get me something nice for Christmas also.

When I finally went to the store and got it I was so happy because, I'd never had to do anything, for anyone in my whole life. Then Christmas came and I could hardly wait to see how surprised she was going to be; when she opened her package from me. I gave my girlfriend a bright red night gown, and she gave me a nice blue shirt. The bad thing about the night gown was I never got see how she looked in it. On the other hand I wore the shirt she'd given me until there was nothing left of it but rags. And every time I wore the shirt I thought about her. But I doubt if she ever did of me, when she wore the night gown.

Our family always went to Pocatello for Christmas to spend the day with my sister Barb and her family for dinner. So on the way to town I had dad drop me off at my girlfriends, house. From here we would come down in her car. I bet we stayed there til 11:00 p. m. or later that night before heading home. However, we often played pinochle throughout the time we spent here, since this was about the only time we got to play cards with my brother in law Roger's family. It was getting late now and I decided it was time to head back toward Blackfoot where I would have my parents pick me up on their way home. So my girlfriend and I told the family good bye and we'd see them later. We finally made it back to my girlfriends, house where I waited for my family to come get me.

It was sometime between Christmas and the New Year when Donetta broke us up. And for a while I didn't know if I wanted to see her again or not. Yet most of the time when I was in town I would go back and see her, but only at the store where she worked. She started out working at one of the hospitals but only in the café part. This was before she got a job at the Big E Store.

At the beginning when I'd take her out I would call her up and say, would" you like to go out to night" and in reply she'd say sure. So I would give her a time over the phone, then say is 8:00 alright. Yes that is fine with me. Next I would be there at the given time that we had agreed on. It varied from time to time since I was helping run the farm with my dad, and my brothers Bob and Paul. There were times when I would call my girlfriend and my family seemed to like interfering with my own business. So when things got this bad I'd end up doing it anyway.

In the meantime my family would tell me you just don't do that sort of thing and a bunch of other stuff. Besides that they were getting on my nerves. I'd already made up my mind and nothing the family could say was going to change that. After I'd taken her out a few times I pretty well knew what her schedule was. She never really had one, and most of the time she didn't know from one minute to the next what she was going to do.

This is what I was trying to point out to the family at the time, so no matter when I would call her, she almost always said yes. But if my girlfriend didn't want to go out that was fine too. I hated to stay at home and often did knowing I'd see Donetta again in a few days. Sometimes I would go to town just to see a friend of mine. When I did stay home I usually spent my time playing pool with dad, or playing mom's dice game Yahtzee with her.

Otherwise I would watch Television to pass the time away, because I got bored a lot at home. This was before I met my girlfriend. But at least when I had one things changed dramatically in my life. There were more things to do, and someone to do them with. So when I moved to Washington and she needed somebody to talk to one night, right after I'd left she went to her mother. And from what I heard Donetta got so lonely that she broke down and cried. I missed her a lot too, the whole time I was gone.

(Revised January 2011)

MY MEMORIES OF UNCLE DOUG

May 12, 2012

One of my most vivid memories that I have of my Uncle Doug goes back to when I was learning how to drive. Well, if you knew my Uncle like I do, you would know how much he liked his old station wagon that he had. I remember when he bought the old Studebaker and that was before I was old enough to drive a car.

Whenever the three families would get together I always noticed where Doug would park his car. It would be in front of my grandmother's house along the side of the white picket fence and always by the gate.

Over a matter of time, all of the kids that grew up on the farm eventually learned to drive our old Farm-all tractors, including me. After I reached my teen age years, I started to help out around the farm during the summer.

What I remember most about those days is haying season. This is when families still helped each other out, back in the 1960's. In spite of having hay fever, I never said no to helping put up hay around the farm. We would go out for a few hours in the morning and work until we thought it was time for lunch and then go home for a spell.

After lunch, we would head back to the hay field and see how much more we could get done before the end of the day. Sometimes I would help my brothers and my cousin, Rich, get the hay off of the field and ready for the farmhand to pick up.

It seems to me as if either my dad or Uncle Fred always operated the farmhand, while the other workers put the stack together starting with the bottom layer and building up. Uncle Doug was never far away or afraid of hard work.

A farmhand is a tractor with a front end loader with several iron teeth across it so it can pick up about 30 bales of hay at one time. From here the person driving the farmhand could bring the hay over to the stackers so they could put the stack together. Many times I remember helping out stacking hay when I wasn't driving one of the tractors for the people slipping the hay.

While I was learning how to drive around the farm I often walked everywhere I went. One day I decided to borrow my dad's yellow pickup and went up to my grandmothers to visit. When I decided to go home, I tried to be as careful as I could backing Dad's truck up on the road and then I heard a small crash. After hearing it, I stopped and got out of the truck to see how bad the damage was.

Well, I'd hit the driver's side door on the old Studebaker Wagon of my Uncle Doug's car but it did not total the car. If I remember right, it was still useable for as long as Doug would drive the darned thing. Eventually the yellow truck and I would show up at home, but I would always feel guilty about the accident I'd caused to the old Studebaker.

MY VISIT TO ALASKA

June 7, 1979

When I went to Alaska to visit my cousins I wasn't sure of what to expect, while I was there. So as soon as I landed in the Anchorage Airport I called my cousin Lloyd and asked him to come and get me. I didn't know how long it would take him to drive out to the airport so I made myself comfortable on the floor while I waited. Finally he showed up, and I was never so glad to see a friendly face in my life.

Hey Lloyd! How are you I said? I'm good he replied. After that we headed to the car so we could go to the house down town where Lloyd and his twin brother Lee and a younger brother Don had grown up. One reason I decided to go see my cousins was because it had been since the late 1960's when they came to visit my family. It was in the middle of November and thirty five degrees below zero in down town Anchorage. I could walk anywhere I wanted to go, while my cousins Lloyd and Don went to work every day.

Probably the most interesting thing while I was there, was when Lloyd took me out to see the glaciers; that were just outside Anchorage up the Seward Highway. I'd never seen anything like it in my entire life. So I was quite taken in by these mountains of ice. On our way back to town I noticed all these abandoned buildings out in the middle of nowhere. At first I didn't know why they were there. Then I finally figured it had to be from the 1964 earth quake, which happened about the same time as the one in California.

I think it might have been this same night when Lloyd showed me what the town of Anchorage looked like after dark. I remember because we were sitting in his pick up on some hill side overlooking the town site. I have to say it was quite a site I told Lloyd while we sat there. He even admitted it and, said I agree with you Bill; in a soft gentle voice.

We were on our way back to the house now so we could find something to eat. We finally got there and as we were entering the house, cousin Don says; hi Bill! How have you been? So I turned to him and said I'm fine. It's been a long time since I've seen you last, I said. Yeah a few years Don commented. One day while I was there Lloyd took me out to see where his homestead was way out in the country side. When we were driving around in the middle of nowhere we never saw any animals. This was a big disappointment to me when I at least expected to see a Brown Bear, or a Moose.

I'd been here for a couple of weeks now and thanksgiving was only a few days away. So I asked my cousins if they had any plans. Which of course they did. Apparently they had some friends, or neighbors, nearby so we went there for Thanksgiving. Throughout the day while we were here I got introduced to a card game called tripoly. This was a different way of playing poker than I'd been used to. Eventually we made our way back to the house after a long day.

One night while I was staying with cousin Don, and Lloyd, I asked Lloyd if I could use the phone. So he gave his permission for me to do so. Right after that I called his twin brother Lee up in Fairbanks. The phone rings, and Lee answers it. Hello he said! So I said hello on the other end Do you know who you're talking to, I said. And he said no. This is when I spoke up and said, I'm your cousin Bill, from Idaho. Oh Lee came back, how are you? And I replied fine.

While we were on the phone I told him, I was staying with his brothers. Throughout our conversation I asked him how cold it was up there. He came back on the phone again then said oh about 60 below zero. From here I decided that was too cold for me. And there was no way I was going to deal with that cold of temperatures. I get off the phone now with Lee even though I'd thought about heading that direction the night before. In doing so I figured my decision was final.

So now I was getting ready to come back home, but before I did I noticed a Billboard down town that read; President Ford was going to be in Anchorage soon. I didn't know how soon or for how long. All I knew was I didn't want to be in the middle of a great big rush. So I left. At first I thought this would be my last chance to see a President. But on the other hand I thought no there will be other times. I have to say it gave me a good feeling inside, and would stay with me the rest of my life; from that point on.

By now I was on my way home on the first flight I could get, out of Alaska and eventually I would be in Seattle, catch the next plane to Walla Walla Washington. After this I would take a bus to Moscow, Idaho then come home with my brother in law Randy, who was going to college at the time.

Revised December 23, 2014

ONE SUMMER MORNING
July 23, 1979

I woke up one morning when it
Was just breaking day light,
Sitting in the big chair
And looking out the window.

On top of the swing set
Were two baby Hoot Owls
Both of them were up there
When I went to move pipe
And they looked so cute, and happy
Just sitting way up there.

Then after pipe when I came home
One of the Owls got scared away,
By the noise of the motor bike.

And the ones that was left
Looked so sad because,
He had lost his friend.

But he stayed until sundown
Then flew away and didn't
Have a care in the world
And went his merry way.

Rewritten October 30, 2014

OUR DOG TROUBLE
Circa 1975

We had an old dog long, long ago
He was the best cow dog you'd ever know,
He'd chase a cow out of the yard without any help
And if he ever got kicked that's when he'd yelp.
My brother found him across the river one day
The year was 1958 and the month was May.

He'd let us kids ride on his back
When we were growing up
I don't know why he did the silly old pup!

He liked to go hunting magpies with me
And chase them all around,
Especially the ones that couldn't fly
That he could kill on the ground.

He'd sleep outside with us
During the summer nights,
And be at the bottom of your sleeping bag
The next morning at sunlight.

He liked to snore that funny old dog
Cause when he slept, he slept like a log.

Although his name was Trouble
He was really no trouble at all,
Because when you would go to the door
He always came when you would call.

He taught Otis to chase a cow just before he died
But even after he did die,
I couldn't help but almost cry.

Because now I'd lost a very good friend
Which his life had now come to an end.
We had a lot of good times ole Trouble and I
And when his time came, I hated to say good bye.

Revised March 12, 2014

OUR TRIP TO SOUTH DAKOTA

July 6, 2003

We were going to have a family reunion
Then something happened along the way,
There came a warning from my cousin
So it took us about two days.

While we were traveling from here to there
We stayed with an old friend of mine,
I asked him if we could spend the night
And he told me that would be just fine.

I said to my friend, we would be gone
And you'd never know we were here
The first thing in the morning
On a day I hoped would be clear.

So here we go down the road again
Toward the great Black Hills,
In a land that once knew no mercy
Where Jack McCall killed Wild Bill.

We finally made our way over there
To the camping spot and stayed,
Where we could hear the whistle blow
Clear down there by the lake.

Oh yes; the train upon the hillside
One day it had caught my eyes,
So the wife and I decided to go
And take our daughter on the long ride.

The train was a fun experience for us
And the ride was an hour each way,
It stopped at a place called Keystone junction
Then back to Hill City for the day.

Every day was a unique one
To be gone all day with my cousin, Dave
And the families that gathered there;
We went to see all these different caves.

There were times when we would go
To see the sites after dark,
Places like the Faces on the Rocks
With a spotlight and under the stars.

We had a fantastic party there
It was the ultimate of all,
Kind of like we do at home,
And all the families had a ball.

But one day we wanted to be alone
Because Melissa had been being good,
This was the day we left her with Aunt Gerry;
While we went to Deadwood.

Here in the town of Deadwood
It seemed as if time stood still,
We stopped at Keven Costner's Restaurant;
And then went to see the graves of
Calamity Jane and Gunfighter Wild Bill.

I don't remember which day it was
During our week long stay,
All I do remember about it was
It happened to be Ana's Birthday.

Rewritten November 8, 2014

PIZZA

November 18, 1978

My little sister likes pizza a lot
She must have a little Italian in her,
There must be something wrong
That the family could cure.

Of course I like it too
Just the same as her,
So something is wrong with me too
And that I know for sure.

She would eat it every day
If she could, and believe me,
Knowing her she would.

We all like it at some time
Or another regardless of Race or creed,
But we are Welshmen and an Italian place
Is one place a Welshman should not be.

Though after a while it gets to you
And you can't stop eating it,
You take one piece after another
Until you're filled to the gullet.

PLAYING POOL

December 12, 1976

I like to play pool a lot
Although I'm not a pro
I have beaten a few people,
But there's still a lot I don't know.

I have watched the professionals play
They make it look so easy to do,
It looks like if they can do it
That you could too.

Rewritten November 8, 2014

SAFETY BREAK SONG
May 24, 1984

We are just a bunch of C.B.ers
Probably the best in the land,
We are just a bunch of C.B.ers
We will give you a helping hand.

Yes if you are down the road
And are stranded out somewhere,
Give us a call on the radio
And we will be on the air.

We are just a bunch of C.B. ers
Trying to help someone out,
And if we are listening to the ole radio
Go ahead and give us a shout.

Drop by and see us if you have time
And have a cup of coffee or two.
Yeah 10- 4 good buddy we have
Punch, hot chocolate and cookies too.

Please sign the book that's on the table
Before you go down the road;
And have a nice trip. See you later
And we will catch you on the flip side, 73's

SPECIAL FRIENDS

August 13, 1978

It's great to have a friend
No matter where you go,
That you can share feelings with
And understands you so.

After all what are friends for
If they can't help each other out,
One can only help another
When one is feeling low or down.

By putting his arm around them
And to show them that he cares,
I'm not talking about any friend
I'm saying girls in particular.

Because other men don't understand
Another man's feeling the way that women do.

Revised September 30, 2013

TELEPHONE OPERATORS
Summer 1978

Whenever you need a friend
Sometimes you can call the Operator,
And she will listen to you.

I tried to get a hold of my sister one night
I must have tried five times.
Although the first time, I got the wrong party.

So I went back and had
Another cup of coffee and,
Then I told the Operator
That I would try again later.

But the next time I tried
I got a different Operator,
It wasn't the same one.

It was the third or fourth time
Before I got the same Operator again.
She seemed very nice, so I told her thanks,
For helping me and I deeply appreciated
All she did for me.

Rewritten May 10, 2014

THE BILL SHOT

July 27, 2011

While Travis and I would play pool
And Little Jenny tended the Bar,
We would play by the hour, and
He was a better player by far.

But there were times when Travis didn't know
What to do when someone put him in a spot,
So I'd take him aside for a minute
And explain to him, you can make that shot.

As we happened to be standing there
And looking at the shot on the table,
I would show Travis how to play it
And of making it, I knew he was capable.

In order to make the shot here
I'd have to shoot it at a difficult angle
And later it gently rolled in the pocket
We would start the game over again;
And put them in the triangle.

After demonstrating the shot I just did!
And watching the ball as it rolls in
We had a right to be a little excited
Because, on our faces we both had huge grin.

The two of us played most of the night

One we won't forget very soon
The lighting couldn't have been any better
Than it was that night in the bar room.

Sometime later when we were playing
I would ask Travis about the shot,
I had showed him so long ago
And he'd say, Bill, let me tell you about that.

Whenever I was working out of town
And someone wanted to play a game,
I would remember the shot you showed me
And later I would give it your name.

THE CAT AND MY HAT

December 18, 1979

The other day when I
Picked up a little kitten
And held it in my arms,
It wanted to cuddle up
So I put it under my chin.

When I didn't want to hold
The kitten anymore,
I'd put it up on my shoulder.

It didn't mind that as long as
You gave it plenty of attention.

I wore my hat all day long
But the kitten didn't like that,
Or for me to have it on.

He'd climb on my neck
And would knock off my hat,
I'd never seen a cat
That would ever do that.

Revised October 21, 2014

THE END OF A SECOND BAD MARRIAGE
July 6, 2011

After having tried the married life
I'm finding that it's not for me,
Because all we ever seem to do;
Is fight all the time which means
I'd be better off being free.

So the thing I have to do now
Is to get my life back on track,
And do things like I used to
And from here on never look back.

We never really had a life together;
The way married people are supposed to
And enjoy each other for a lifetime;
Instead of throwing up ones arms
And then saying I'm though.

This is what seems to happen when
Two partners aren't meant for each other,
Then eventually they wind up divorced;
And go their separate ways because
This decision was one that was forced.

Our lives will on as usual
And I'm not missing anything by getting out,
Because there never was any love for me
And this I really have no doubt.

By ending another bad marriage
The only thing that I'd have to look for,
Are the good times I'd have going to town
And not worrying about a wife anymore.

So this is where I'm going to close
The chapter on my married life,
And go back to the way I was
Before I ever thought about having a wife.

THE FARMERS STRIKE
Summer 1979

It's about time the farmers had their way
When everybody else always gets their way.
They never know when to sell their crops
For usually when they want to, the market drops.

With the prices of cattle these days
You can't afford to feed them expensive hay.
It's been a long time since the farmers made anything
And when they did, it wouldn't buy a new machine.

No, the farmers can't afford to take a loss
At the price of what new machinery costs.
But they have to anyway,
Whether or not they have a say.

Like when a buyer comes to look at your stuff
You know what he offers you, won't be enough.

It wouldn't be so bad if they
Could keep from going broke,
But to the public, it's all a big joke.

They think, aw what do we care?
But to the farmers, that isn't being fair.

THE GOOD DEED DOERS

January 30, 2012

I was headed to work one morning
Like I'd done so many times before,
It was right in the middle of winter;
And going to work as it was
Seemed to be quite a chore.

We'd had a really bad winter that year
And I was buying a brand new truck,
When a couple of my friends came along
And they could see that I was stuck.

So here I was stranded on some road
Where I'd buried the truck to the bones,
And I was glad my friends came along
Since I'd just gotten off the phone.

My friends and I tried to pull me out
As I am waiting for help to show up,
That would cost me an arm and a leg later
And I was already so mad that I could shout.

While all this bologna was going on
My friends had gone to work by now,
And the Cop who'd been watching me
Didn't even try to make an effort, somehow.

Somewhere in the midst of this commotion
I called my work and told them I'd be in,
As soon as I got out of this snow bank
And I think that was close to 10:00.

THE LONG JOURNEY
October 23, 2013

I remember one time when my sister Gerry came to visit us, after she and Bill Becker had been married for a short time. The reason Beautiful Bill wasn't with Gerry was, because he was in California on business. I was still living with mom and dad at the time, and sometime later I would get a present that Gerry's husband got me while he was in California.

The family and I didn't know how long Beautiful Bill was going to be gone, so we came up with a plan to take my sister back to Washington. So on our great adventures as we start out from home, it was Mom, Dad, Uncle Doug my sister Gerry and myself. For a while we got along with dad's car quite well, but later would have problems with it or so it seems to me and my sister.

Gerry agrees with me too that this was around 1976 after our Grandmother had died; otherwise Uncle Doug wouldn't have been able to go with us. We had been on the road for some time now and it was going to be dark soon. Somewhere between Boise, Idaho and Baker, Oregon we finally had trouble with the car we were driving.

While we were sitting in the car I was trying to come up with an idea to be of some use here. Finally it came to me. I said to myself Bill "get out on the side of the road and wave down the truck drivers." So I did. God only knows how long it took before I finally got one to actually stop. And when they did I noticed the name of the company on the side of the truck. North American Van Lines. Were we ever glad he came along when he did. So when he came to a stop and asked me what the problem was, I told him our car wouldn't start, and we needed towed so someone could look at it. From here he would get on the radio and call somebody to come and rescue us.

They finally came with the tow truck and were hooking it up to dad's car. In the meantime I was thanking the truck driver for helping us out so he could get on his way to his destination. Our journey was far from over and we would be in Baker, Oregon soon where we could look at dad's car. Once we got there we put the car in the shop where we could have the person who rescued us give us an idea of what the problem was. After he had looked over the car he finally came to the conclusion that we needed a new fan belt.

So after all the trouble we'd been through, we were now on our way to Walla Walla to take my sister Gerry home. Eventually we would wind up in this town and spend a few days while we were here. The next day we went and bought some building materials down town and went back to Gerry's place and proceeded to build her and her husband a water bed. This was back when water beds were very popular in the 1970's. After getting the lumber and taking it back to Gerry's, then we began to cut what we had to the proper length so we could put it together. This was one project I really had fun helping out with. Once it was put together the rest of us would come back home.

THE ROOSTER FIGHT

March 11, 1980

We were driving through Oregon
Just My friend and I
And on the way home we happened
To be driving over the 4th of July.

We missed the turn off at La Grande
And went way out in the hills.

Along the way we would look at
The scenery while driving by,
Then on a hill side that we saw;
Were three rooster pheasants
And I thought, what a beautiful sight.

So we stopped and watched them
For a little while, and then
Two of them would begin to fight
For a few minutes and quit;
And start all over again.

The third rooster pheasant he decided
I don't want any part of that!
So he just stayed out of the way
And let them have their spat.

THE SALMON RIVER

June 21, 1975

There is a river that runs in Idaho
Where people have lost their lives.

Boating, fishing, swimming
And having lots of fun,
Until the unexpected happens
And they are no more.

Because of something they forgot
That they shouldn't have before.

That one thing could have
Saved a lot of lives,
If people would just think twice.
Oh yes, the life jacket!
Why didn't I think of that!

Well we'll, risk it this time
But not again they say,
And drown in that terrible river;
And are statistics in the newspaper
The very next day.
Because that river won't give
People a second chance.

THE SESQUICENTENNIAL OF THE OREGON TRAIL WAGON TRAIN: 1843-1993

July 17, 2012

I remember an article of an event that was going to happen soon so I asked my family what they thought of it. And of course all of us thought it was an excellent idea. One reason we gave a lot of thought to this was it probably wouldn't ever happen again in my lifetime or my parents. Well, before I get too far into this story I better tell you what happened up to this point. I'd been married once before to a local girl back in the 1980's. I thought she would be good for me but she turned out to be a real dud even though she came from a good family. All of her brothers and sisters liked me, and I got where I liked them as well. Her dad and I became very good friends over the years even the three bad ones that I was married to his daughter Mary, before getting a divorce from her.

So after a while I started hanging out at the bars again and I would run into someone I knew from back in the 1970's. A few years go by now after my divorce was final and I would ask Joe Harris if he still had a daughter living at home. And of course he did, but I didn't know because I had just moved back home from Walla Walla Washington in 1979. So I had a guaranteed job working for my dad and my brothers again and a place to stay; because my dad had bought a trailer house for my first wife and me and put it on the farm. While I was working for the farm seven days a week I would only go out on Friday and Saturday nights; looking for a woman to have a good time with or someone to play pool with. Sometimes I would find both.

A couple of years go by after my divorce I'd been working at a local potato warehouse, so now I had my own money; and I didn't feel guilty about relying on the farm anymore. At this point in my life the only thing lacking was that sense of security one gets when they have someone to share their life with. Well, all my family knew what this feeling was like but I didn't. So now I started going out with Joe Harris's daughter again hoping that things would be better between us than they were in the 1970's. Donetta still worked at the store in town where she'd been since I'd met her the first time. So we went out for about a year before we decided to get married.

The day finally got here that we'd been looking forward to that would bring the two families together. And the family I was marrying into didn't have a clue how big of a family I came from until we actually got together. After the wedding was over and done with I'd never seen so many people in all my life in the backyard of my wife's parents place. I don't remember how many we had invited to come, but I had invited a special friend that I had worked with for a few years at the plant in Firth.

I never did know my friends name but the people we worked for called him Chief. So all these years the only name I've ever known my friend by was Chief. If I remember right Chief and his family were one of our first guests to come to the reception, and I was very glad to see them. From here I would go back to work until I would get laid off in July, then we could take our honeymoon. While I was working at my job, my now wife was still working at the store where she'd been since she started in 1976.

During this same time my youngest sister was working as a counselor in Northern Idaho so the family had to wait for her to come home. Well, somewhere in between times of her coming home from Moscow, we'd had one kid. She was two years old at the time of the 150 anniversary of the Oregon Trail. At this time, I would try to read the newspaper whenever possible so I always knew what was going on. In the meantime my wife and I would work at our jobs until the day of the actual event.

My sister finally made it home for the summer so we could start putting our plans together to go meet the wagon train, which wasn't that far to drive from where we lived. July 4th a bunch of us decided we would get in the car and head out. Dad was driving while the rest of us talked back and forth as we were traversing on our way. Mom's sister Virginia was with us, along with my second wife and our two year old daughter at the time. Well, somewhere along the way my dad came to a complete stop. And if you knew my dad the way I do, you would know that it would take one absolute reason to do such a thing. But being the person he is; he did have probable cause to stop.

While we were stopped dad got out to see what the matter was. The family and I waited patiently for a decision from my father, while he was checking things out. So we drove through the water that held us up in the first place; and as we do so we dragged the bottom of the car. Now that we were across the wash we would continue on our way to see the wagon train. I don't remember how long it was before we reached our destination at a place called Alkali Flats that was just up the reservation.

What's odd about this situation is, it was right on the original Oregon Trail so it had a double meaning for me. We finally got where we were headed and got out of the car, stretched our legs for a bit walking around, and seeing what kind of stuff they had for sale up there. While we were up here dad and I would talk to the teamsters, check out their wagons, and admire the beautiful horses that pulled the wagons. Overall I bet we spent about two hours here before we wound up in Pocatello at my sister Barb's house for a while that night before coming back home. This is one time I can truly say I really had a good time because I helped organize this expedition.

THE TETON DAM

June 5, 1976

The Teton Dam was a terrible thing to happen the way it did. It drowned Sugar City, Rexburg, and all the Roberts, Menan country. I had friends who lived in the Menan area at the time, and it really wiped them out. But at that time, they told me they needed a bigger house anyway; because their other one was just too small.

My folks, my sister, her husband, his parents and I had been in the area of the Teton Dam the day before, the flood happened. From what we could tell when we drove by it is, it didn't look that serious; even though there was a small leak in the earth made dam. So we thought nothing of it. This was on our way up the country to Jenny's Lake which lies on the outskirts of Jackson Hole Wyoming. I'm sure everybody had a good time including my sister's in-laws Dan and Margaret.

I was very glad to see the Becker's and be able to spend the day with them, as I'm sure my parents were too. Since most of the time we were great distances apart, because of different areas that separated us in Idaho. The next day Saturday June 5th 1976 I had been cutting hay for my brothers down by the river for a while; before going to the house for lunch. This is when mom asked me if I wanted to go watch the flood waters go through Firth. So I just said yes. By now everybody in the upper and lower Snake River Valley had heard about the breaking of the Teton Dam, including me. And I heard about it over the radio and television. When I saw poor Rexburg, and Sugar City, I felt sorry for those people who didn't have a home anymore. This is when I knew Firth and Blackfoot were right along the river that was flooding; so I wondered what might happen to them.

While the flood waters were making their way through town other parts had found its way through canals west of town, where my dad's brother lived; along with other neighbors of his that we knew. And yes, it really damaged that side of Firth that was formally known as Lava Side. There was one good thing that came out of this whole ordeal of The Teton Dam. And that was, if it had happened at night instead of the day time; more people would have lost their lives. As it was I think maybe a total of eleven lives were lost.

Here was my home town where I had gone to school and now it was practically floating away. I couldn't believe what I saw. The road that went down to the High School was completely washed out, and the water was so high; it covered some mobile homes. The day after the flood happened I went over to see what was left of my town.

Revised Dec 23, 2014

THE WAR WITH IRAQ: A MESSAGE TO SADDAM

March 27, 2003

I can't believe you want this war
One you know you can't win.
And indulge yourself and your people
In terror, fright, and sin.

Had you only obeyed the rules,
Of the International Laws
We wouldn't be where we are
And you are the justified cause.

You can have your rabble rousers,
You can have your outlaw band-
But you won't have anything,
As long as George Bush is in command.

Let this be a lesson to you,
One you need to learn well,
Because we are the American Army
And we will blow your Outlaws to Hell.

I do support our country,
And our Commander in Chief.
I think he's doing a great job,
But that might be my own personal belief.
Your people need to learn to live
In peace and understand.
Lay your guns upon the ground,
And live by God's command.

To The Iraqi People:

Give up your violent way of life
That you have lived so long,
And accept the life of freedom
Get out from under Saddam.

Saddam is a man of evil,
The wicked, unrighteous, you know.
You do not want to follow him
Or to go where he may go.

If you think you can run away
And that you won't be found,
I believe that you are wrong;
Because our troops will find you
In the air or on the ground.

We have the mightiest Navy ships
That can hit you where you stand.
And our Patriot missiles will hit your scuds
Which were supposed to be banned.

It does not matter where you travel
In that desert or out on the sand,
And the minute that you turn your back
We will wipe out your contraband.

A day will come when you least expect,
To be surrounded by our tanks.
And when the war is over
The U.S. people you will thank.

Soon there won't be anywhere
For you to run and hide,

Because your boundaries will be narrowed
And not so far and wide.

Then there is that other one
Who thinks he knows it all,
You know who I'm talking about
The bearded one who is so tall.

One day he will be going
And lucky he will not be,
Running through Afghanistan,
And into American Infantry.

And when this whole thing is over
With our enemies out of the way,
We won't have to live in terror
And their games we will not play.
I'm looking for the day to come
When the troops come home again,
So the world can live in peace,
And someone else we don't have to defend.

Rewritten December 2, 2014

THE WORKAHOLIC

November 18, 1978

The workaholic is someone
Who is willing to work,
And sometimes, those who don't.

He or she is devoted to
The job that they have,
Or had at one time.

In their line of work they have to
Get along with the people they're around.

And if they don't like the job
That they currently have,
They should find something they do like
Instead of going on and on.

A workaholic is people from
Every walk of life.
Almost any place you look
You will find people who want to work.

The farmer is devoted to his work
As a waitress is to hers.
There are times when they would rather
Do something else its true.

Because everyone needs a break
From their job no matter what it is,

The workaholic is the man or woman
Who bend over a lot and are sore,
At the end of a long day.

He's the mechanic that repairs your car
Or the nurse who draws your blood.

The workaholic isn't someone
Who gets hired and works for
A few minutes and takes a break,
Starts working again;
And does the same thing
Over and over, time and again.

Revised August 11, 2014

TO LEON AND ANNE

August 1981

I hope both of you much happiness
Throughout your married life
And I'm sure that Anne will
Make you a fine wife.

Share everything together
The best way that you can,
And make all of your decisions
So that you both understand.

I wouldn't want to intervene
And see either of you hurt,
It isn't all that easy to
Make a marriage work.

Think of me once in a while
For writing this note,
I will always be your friend
And for you this is what I wrote.

Revised October 21, 2014

TO MILES ANDERSON
Circa 1978

I admire you a lot
For what you've done for me,
Not only for talking to, but
Also for the company.

I feel that I can come to you
Whenever I have a problem,
That the two of us could solve
Together without involving anyone.

I tell you what I think
And you do the same in return.
But the other day when you
Called me Mister Reid,
I didn't mind at all.

But, I'm not the Duke of Windsor
Or the Earl of Denmark,
I'm not the King of Scotland
Or the Prince of Wales.

I'm not King Edward the VII
Or King George the VI,
What I'm trying to say is;
You can call me by my name.

TOTAL ECLIPSE

March 6, 1979

On February 26, 1979
I witnessed an eclipse of the sun.
When I went to work that day
The dawn was just breaking,
And the birds were getting up.

Then twenty minutes later
It started to get dark again.

Street lights were coming on
Cars were turning their lights on too,
And even the birds went back to bed
Because they didn't know what was up.

It was really too cloudy to see very much
And it was like midnight all over again
Except without the moon and the stars.

I was standing outside the door
Of the place where I was working,
When the whole thing took place.

TRAILS WEST: NO. 14

November 4, 1975

There are no more trails to follow
There are no more prairies to cross,
There are no more trail drives to go on
With the head man the trail boss.

There are no more fortunes to seek
And no more discoveries to be found,
Like gold was when the
Pioneers came west bound.

Yes, the pioneers, the era of the west
A time in history I like the very best.

Revised June 12, 2014

UNCLE FRED'S 93RD BIRTHDAY
February 5, 2012

Happy Birthday to my Uncle Fred
Every time I turn around you amaze me
And I have a hard time believing,
You're now the incredible age of 93.

When it seems as only yesterday
We were trailing our cows to the hills
And now you get a second birthday poem
From one of your nephews named Bill.

One of the last roundups I remember
Of helping you bring your cows, home,
After we'd gotten them all rounded up
There was one old sheep out here all alone.

And here it was as happy as can be
Trailing behind a bunch of cows
Even when we got them home
It just seemed to fit in somehow.

So once again I have to say
Thanks for the wonderful memories
And being a big part of my life
Have a terrific 93rd Birthday.

UNCLE FRED'S 85TH BIRTHDAY

March 21, 2004

I'm sorry we missed your party
And an invite we didn't need,
I would have stayed a little longer
But I didn't want to impose upon
The family of the Fred Reid's.

I hated to leave like I did you see
And I'd only have been in the way,
With everyone coming like they were
After all, it was Uncle Fred's birthday.

So it was better I just drop by
Since this is the kind of person I am,
You have to check in once in awhile;
Or the elderly in the family will
Think that you are being shy.

I remember Fred back in the days
When we still put up hay by hand,
Especially the summer I broke my leg
And My cousin, Lloyd happened to be;
The farm's number one man.

My cousin, Janene, happened to be there
When from the haystack I did fall,
And she was the one who took me home
Because there was no way for my folks to call

HAPPY 84TH BIRTHDAY UNCLE WALLACE
April 2, 2013

Well, I always did like my Uncle Wallace, and
I almost had to. In the first place he gave me a job
Right out of high school. I did not have a driver's
License yet, but I could drive anything on the farm,
Including our trucks and tractors.

But the job I would remember the most and
Wallace would too, is when we would go out on the
Road with his potato cutter for his customers,
Wherever we might be headed. Sometimes these jobs
Were in local areas like Blackfoot or Shelley and other
Times they were out of town.

Eventually, I would get my driver's license and
I did, but not until 1974. After that there was a
Whole world that opened up for me. Not only for going
Out on weekends, but for hauling anything from the
Farm to town. You never knew what you were
Going to be hauling except during the summer or fall.

I always looked forward to helping Wallace out
Every April and he knew he could count on me.
Well, in the beginning it was just Wallace, his
Son-in-law, Steve Blaser, and myself for a
Few years. But no matter whether we were
Going to work or on the way home; we always
Had to have our Russian Tea that Mom would
Make for me.

I always tried to make myself available for
Wallace during the summer when I wasn't working
For my brothers. This way I could help Wallace hauling
His wheat, barley, oats, or whatever to town to help my
Uncle out wherever I could.

Some things happen sometimes in families, and
Often do, they have a falling out and go their separate
Ways. This is what happened to my cousin, Debbie
And her husband, the lawyer.

I don't exactly remember when Wally was looking for
Another hired man for full time help, but I do
Remember when a young punk kid out of California
Showed up at my Uncle Wallace's door looking for
Work. Everybody knew who the kid was anyway
Because his family had previously lived out here in
The valley.

So for the next few years, I would work for Wallace
And try to get to know his new hired hand. I have
To say that Blake the Snake was a totally different
Person right from the beginning. You never knew from
One day to the next what he was going to do or say.
And you didn't want to be in the same vehicle with him
If you didn't have to be.

The reason I know this is because he and I had been
Working one day for my uncle and I think Wallace
Wanted us to go to town to get something for him. We
No more got out of my uncle's driveway and at the top
Of the road when I heard this noise, plop, plop, plop. So
I said "Blake, I think you better pull over". And we did
After we came to a stop.

We both jumped out of Blake's pickup and immediately
Started to get the jack, lug wrench and other stuff out of
Blake's pickup to take the flat tire off of his truck and get
The spare on a.s.a.p. In the meantime, he was cussing up one
Side and down the other. I'd never heard such bad language
In all my born days. Not even from my dad or his brothers

We finally got the tire on the pickup and on our way to town
So we could finish the task we set out to do in the first place.
I don't remember how long Blake had worked for my family
Before he decided to get married. The funny part about this
Story is my family and I already knew the girl Blake was
Going to marry.

My family had gotten acquainted with Denise through
Farmers Insurance Group in Blackfoot. The farm machinery
Was already insured with this company and it only made
Sense to have our cars and pickups on the same plan for
One low price. So, for many years the family stayed with
This insurance until they decided they were no longer going
To work with the family.

Even though we were no longer with the insurance that
Denise worked for, the families kept in touch. In fact, If
There was something going on in the valley, Blake and
Denise were not very far away, especially after they had a
Couple of kids. The two of them liked showing off what
They had.

It was not hard to tell for anyone that those two were sure
Meant for one another. I don't know how many years over-all
That Blake worked for Wallace but I'm sure he deeply appreciated
The person who showed up on that one particular day.

One of the most vivid memories I have of Marlene and Wallace
Is when Ken and Becky got married over in what we always called
The lower field. This was a small portion of land with a huge
Grove of trees that my Uncle Fred owned. It was a short distance
From where my oldest brother and his wife lived, just a hop,
Skip and a jump away.

So, when Ken and Becky decided to get married I was glad
When they chose this location to get married in. For the most part,
It was convenient for anyone who lived out here in the valley. But
For people who came a long ways away like Mom's family in
California, it probably seemed like forever getting here. It was
Only a matter of days now before the big wedding would happen.
After all, we were waiting on a couple of Ken's friends to get
Here from California.

The big day was finally here that would bring the Reid Family and
The Davis family together for the second time. While those of us
Who lived here in the valley only had a short drive to the Lower
Field, others had to drive great distances from out of town.
By this time most people were finding a
Parking spot for the ceremony.

I didn't have to worry about finding a girl for the event because I'd
Already asked my friend Lori from Blackfoot. Just before the
Ceremony, I looked out in the distance and saw some horseback
Riders coming. It was the Wallace Reid Family. The next thought
I had was, how original this could be. And especially for Ken and
Becky's wedding on that September day in 1977.

WILD BILL HICKOK
Circa 1976

Wild Bill Hickok was quite a Marshal
In the old Wild West
In fact you might say
He was the very best.

Although Abilene's people didn't
Like Gun toting any,
With all the shootings and killings
Which there must have been many.

Between the James Gang
And the Wild Bunch,
Ole Wild Bill, he had a hunch.

Until one day when he was slain
By Jack McCall during a poker game.
Because Jack McCall knew if he
Got Wild Bill out in the street,
That the end would come for him
And he would be beat.

And because Wild Bill was the law
Everyone knew he was quick on the draw.

Revised March 20, 2014

WRITERS NO. 10

February 4, 1976

Being a writer is one thing
Getting there is another,
That's why I'd like to be
Like my Grandmother.

She's written three books
I haven't written any,
But that's not to say I won't;
The time will come some day
We'll be in the same boat.

Revised June 11, 2014

ACKNOWLEDGEMENT

January 23, 2015

I would like to thank a few people who helped
Me put my first book together;
Starting with my two younger sisters, Gerry,
And Ginger, for their part helping type
My stories, and with proof reading. Next I have
To say, thanks to my niece, Stacey,
For having the files she did have on hand. And
Now, a great big thank you to my
cousin, Becky, because without her the picture
wouldn't be on the back of my
first book.

Written By
William D. Reid

www.ingramcontent.com/pod-product-compliance
Lightning Source LLC
Chambersburg PA
CBHW021643120626
46545CB00002B/679